CLEAR! Breathing Life, Duplication & Simplicity
Into Your Network Marketing Business:
With TOP SECRET Tips To Automate Your Teams Growth!

Sean Gary

CLEAR! Breathing Life, Duplication & Simplicity Into Your Network Marketing Business: With TOP SECRET Tips To Automate Your Teams Growth!

Copyright © 2018 By Sean C. Gary

Printed in the United States of America

First Printing 2018

ISBN-13: 978-1726124973
ISBN-10: 1726124975

All rights reserved. No part of this publication may be reproduced, scanned, or transmitted in any form, digital or printed, without the definitive written permission of the Author.

www.SeanGary.com

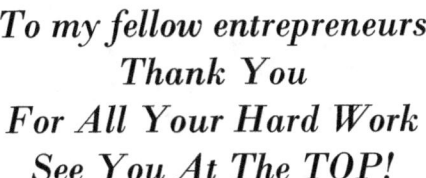

To my fellow entrepreneurs
Thank You
For All Your Hard Work
See You At The TOP!

Dear Reader,

First, I just want to say thank you for taking time to grow you! I wrote this book for you, the person who joined a Network Marketing company and didn't really know where to go from there.

Personally, I decided to write a book that everyone in my personal organization would be able to purchase and then distribute to every single new rep or affiliate that they signed up. No more would I sit back and watch people struggle to understand what this industry is and how to maximize this blessing.

I hope that you are fired up and more than anything I hope that you are ready to take notes (you can do that in the back of this book in the workbook section). If you are these things, then lastly, I hope that you are coachable and ready to be successful in this industry.

My promise to you is that you will have the information to understand the basics of Network Marketing and that you will grab hold of the simple duplicatable system in the workbook section that will help you grow your business and help others to do the same.

Hang in and hold tight! We have many people to bless. After myself, (blessed that you are taking time to read my research and notes) secondly, I believe you will be blessed.

Now let's get started!

Your
Coach, Friend & Brother...
Sean Gary The Success Jolt

Table of Contents

Section I

Welcome	1
My Story	3
Why Network Marketing?	9
Five Keys to Success	15
Cold Market Vs. Warm Market	25
Most Important Fact About Building	29
Ways to Share	31
Determine Your Goals	33
Personal Development	35
Duplication	39

Section II

Notes	43
Fast Start Game Plan	49
System 1 Warm Market	51
Scripts: 3-Way Calls	55
Closing	59
About the Author	61

Clear! Breathing Life, Duplication & Simplicity

Section I

Welcome

First off, I want to thank you! I'm not thanking you just for purchasing this book, I'm thanking you for taking a chance on something new; I'm thanking you for betting on you! It is essential to understand that you have just moved closer to building your dreams and being able to live a lifestyle that many have dreamed of, but never took a step towards obtaining. You have, so not just a thank you is due, but a Major CONGRATULATIONS!

So now that we have that taken care of, understand that this industry can be robust, it can be very tough. When you join a team that has no structure or system, and the leadership is vacant, it can be complicated to get going. You have likely heard this by now, but you currently are in business FOR YOURSELF BUT NOT BY YOURSELF! So that means you may have help, but there are no excuses.

Your success is not going to be determined by your upline sponsor, or the fact that your team doesn't have a website, or they

Sean Gary

don't have weekly meetings in your area. This is a business, and you are the owner. Currently, you are in complete control of the direction in which your business goes. It's been said by a wise man, you cannot control what happens to you, but you can control how you respond to it. Another one I like, though it may seem a little harsh is, you can't control where you were born, but you can affect where you die.

Take that to heart as you begin to grow your business. When it comes to people joining your team, your business, remember "some will, some won't, so what?" We must continue to press, getting better through personal development and coaching. As that happens, we will hear less "no's" and begin to hear more "yeses"! This industry is not perfect, but I think it's the best one!

My Story

I remember it like it was yesterday. I was wiping tables, moving quickly preparing for the lunch rush. It was the summer of 2005, and I was home from school. The next year I would be a Junior at Tiffin University. I was a server at Apple Bee's, a restaurant in Columbus, Ohio. It was like a usual rush; tons of people came in and were in a hurry. Usually, orders were requested to be put in quickly so that they could get back to work on time.

As the rush slowed down and the restaurant cleared out, I noticed a small group of about 6-8 individuals. It was something about them that drew my attention. It could have been that they were, as they say, "dressed to impress" or "suited and booted." But neither one of those sayings that described their clean business look sparked my curiosity. One could confidently suggest that it was the fact that they were also minorities like myself that had drawn my

Sean Gary

attention. That idea also would receive a failing grade if it were a test.

What had me focused more intently on them and their visit was that they were all still laughing and eating and even ordering more food. I was not sure where they worked, but it appeared to me that they had jobs that didn't care about them returning from lunch on time. Usually, there was a clearing out of the restaurant, and they didn't seem to budge as everyone else appeared to pay their checks and leave.

Having the inquisitive mind that I had and that I still have today, I decided to approach them and see. I felt that there was something special about them and I wanted to know what it was! I walked over self-assuredly and respectfully asked "What is it that you all do? Everyone else has left, and you all are still here."

That's when one of them looked across the table and nodded to the other guy as if saying, "go ahead, you take him." I could smile later because I would come to understand that they were letting "BIG MIKE", who stood about 5 feet 5 and a half inches tall, come to share the opportunity with me and sign me up! Everything I heard sounded great, and I was impressed with this world that I was watching before my eyes.

The truth is, I signed up right there on the spot. While still on the clock. I was very excited to be connected to what looked like an "ELITE" group of people. I felt lucky, blessed even, to have connected with them.

On my emotional ride home, the thought about how much money I could make crossed my mind a few times, what excitement! More times, however, I thought about learning everything I could from the guys, very eager I was. And the real reality is that I also thought a few times about these strangers that I just had given my social security number and credit card information to. That added a scared and nervous emotion! I laugh about it now, but that day changed my life for the better.

I went for months reading every book suggested and attended every single event and party after the party. I didn't want an opportunity to pass where I had a chance to be close to these guys

Sean Gary

and miss it. I met a ton of other people. Many of which I still know today, and my personal development grew and grew and grew some more. While at that time I had not made one red cent!

I will never forget a friend of mine to this day, a major leader back then, Mr. Marlon Hurd. He was in the parking lot, and he pulled me over and congratulated me on all my successes. I shared with him that I had not made a single dollar yet. He then looked me in my face with extreme surprise and said, "Are you serious?" I told him I was, and he said to me "I have seen you at every event. I have seen you taking notes. I have watched you holding some of the books that we have suggested as great reads. If you are telling me that you have put in this much dedication and have not made any money yet…" this is the main part I never forgot. He continued "… you are gonna crush this industry wide open. You are going to make a TON OF MONEY!!"

I asked him to explain, and he said that most people want a quick fix. They don't wait for the reward from the growth. He said most people don't grow; they don't read, they don't take notes, and they don't stay around if they don't make money right away. He then walked off and told me that I was going to be "Dangerous." I can gladly say that a month or so later, I went back to college and for the first time experienced what it felt to make over $1,000 in a weekend! The rest is history STILL IN THE MAKING!!

Sean Gary

Why Network Marketing?

I previously claimed that this is the best industry. I proclaimed that mainly because of the benefits. I started this book with a welcome that highlighted some of the difficulties. Many won't tell you the hard parts; they will only tell you about the great things about the industry. I made sure to hit a few of those things right off the top.

Sometimes the teams we end up on don't support us as we would like them to. But as an owner of your company you need to be able to not only grind and work hard, but you should enjoy the benefits that the industry provides as well. These are the top 3 reasons I absolutely love this industry!

Freedom

I love the fact that as I increase my income, I can spend more time with my family. I knew, when I was young, that I wanted to have a family. So, I dreamed that I would have plenty of income to provide

Sean Gary

for them. I also imagined I would own my own business and it would allow me the flexibility to come and go as I pleased. This industry can do that for sure.

If you work hard, even if part-time, you can create a residual income that will bless your presence monthly. That income can even grow to replace your jobs income at some point. If you already are an entrepreneur, then this just adds to your freedom and you may already enjoy a different level of freedom that others who are not self-employed don't get to experience.

I'd like to add a side note here, if you are working a job that you love and that you feel God has called you to work, then I would suggest you don't quit. I'd suggest that you use this new income to pay your bills and any debt, which can lower possible stresses in your life. Maybe let it take you on an extra vacation, or on your first vacation.

I don't suggest leaving a situation where you are able to serve others, and you get a great deal of satisfaction from it. A lot of positions that call for serving, in my opinion, usually don't pay very well, so this industry can still help provide freedom for those who serve on their jobs and love it.

Finances

I love the fact that as I improve my skills and increase my value as a person and a leader, there's no one who I must ask if it's okay for me to earn more money. This is the only industry, to my knowledge, that you can walk up to someone making more money than you in the organization and ask them to show you how to make what they make, and they respond with excitement and are excited to do so.

In a traditional company trying to ask your supervisor to make what they make, can place a target on your back. In that moment, you can become competition to them because now they may be threatened by you and your drive to become more valuable in the company. The idea can arise, in their mind, that your desire to "move up" in the company may happen with you taking their position. In the traditional corporate world, you are typically not paid for what you are worth; you are paid for what the position pays. There are moments, however, when you can request a raise outside of what your position pays, but much of the time your financial compensation will remain within the parameters of the budget allocated for that position.

Personal Development

This industry introduced me to the importance of personal development. When it comes to personal development, I love that this industry will allow you to earn as much money that matches the value you bring. I'll speak more on this later in the Personal Development section. I think that everyone has the chance to be a leader. Some are born with leadership traits, but leaders can be made as well.

I feel that every leader in this industry, at one point or another, has given personal development tools to other affiliates on their team. I know personally, I have given some of these same tools to many affiliates who were on other teams as well. But I have even given some personal development links, books, tools, software, invitations to special training etc. to individuals who were not *even* in the Network Marketing industry. It's important to be able to grow

and this industry encourages this!

Sean Gary

Five Keys to Success

What should you bring to the table? What do you need to do to be successful in this industry? I believe there are 5 keys to being successful in this industry. When you combine these 5 keys I believe you position yourself to do 3 things: help a ton of people, have an enormous amount of fun, and generate a massive income. Those first 2 things should always be present, and they will bring the third one with them. The 5 keys for you, however, are being coachable, being hungry, having a short-term memory, using third-party tools and last but one of the most important ones, in my opinion, is having a true desire to help other people!

Be Coachable

It can be easy to respond to someone by saying "I know" after they share information with us or guides us or directs us. I think this response can come because we don't want to be embarrassed or feel like everyone else in the room already knew the information. We feel

Sean Gary

as though we don't want anyone to judge us. We don't want anyone to say we don't belong, or that we are not smart enough. Instead of saying "ok" we agree as if we already know what the trainer knows.

In my experience honesty comes from a place of humility, a place even of integrity. It's best to learn by listening and by taking notes. Those notes ultimately lead to us being able to grow. When we are coachable, it's like providing an empty glass for someone else to pour fresh water into. The water should flow naturally and uninterrupted into the glass. Every time we say "I know" or don't listen, or go against the coaching or training, it's like shaking the glass around which stops all the water from reaching the glass and it also can send some water back out of the glass.

See, understand something, when we can let the coach, coach and let the leader lead, we will be able to get to our destination much quicker. When a new affiliate joins a team and feels like they're not going to listen to the leaders, mentors or uplines, the instructions or direction or not follow the system, it usually ends with both sides being frustrated and no one benefitting. Being coachable increases your chances of having immediate success in this industry.

Be Hungry

When I say be hungry, I hope you understand that it has nothing to do with food. When a person stays hungry, they remain interested and engaged in whatever it takes to help themselves get better. Staying hungry means you're never satisfied with mediocrity.

You want to read one more book, you want to take one more session at the conference, you want 10 more minutes to pick the brain of the leader you are listening to. In this industry, if you stay hungry to be better, you will have a chance to be tremendously successful in this industry.

Have Short-Term Memory

Having a short-term memory is not a bad thing in the terms that I am referring to. I don't like to say that we are in sales, but many would argue that. I would say yes, it is sales, but my goal is not to "sell" someone. My goal (as explained in my Sales Series on YouTube) is to share information. My job is not to tell you what to buy; my job

Sean Gary

is to connect with you and see what it is that you need and try to find the solution to that need.

After finding out what those needs are, I can provide some options that would satisfy the need. What's certain is that after I share the solution it's time for the prospect to decide to purchase or not. I must remember a quick saying... "some will, some won't, so what?" I believe Jim Rohn may have said that one as well. Another way to say it is, "we are looking for the lookers." We are looking for someone who also is looking for us.

Within this industry, we end up sharing our information with prospects who are not "lookers." We share with the "some won't" prospects. If this happens, we must be able to hear those prospects decline our product or service offer, and then say "Thanks" and be able to move on. Short-term memory is merely the art of just getting back on the horse after the horse knocks you off. You never lose until you stop fighting. If nine people knock me down, I don't lose unless I decide not to get back up.

Using Third-Party Tools

Here I will map out the importance of using third party tools or simply using a third person when it comes to sharing your presentation. First off, let's look at using third party tools. What is that you ask? Third party tools are things like: Books, DVDs, CDs or even YouTube videos that are used to share your business opportunity. This is extremely powerful because while your prospect is watching the material, they see the company, they see the video, they see the book. They don't see you!

Most of us make the mistake of "BEING THE GUY"! Don't be the guy, be the guy that introduces the guy! Just provide them with the tool and let the tool share for you!

Some of you are starting in this industry for the first time. This may be your first business ever. If that is the case, and you are sharing this great income opportunity with your prospect, who knows you personally, how would that prospect believe you are going to

Sean Gary

make a ton of money when you still owe them $20 from last Christmas?

It's likely; however, they won't believe you or even take the time to try to understand what you're into. We need to remove ourselves and let the third-party tool speak for us. They will be more excited about what the company is doing and interested in what the company is selling.

Now on to explaining using a third *person* to share for you. Let's look at a situation where an individual, very well spoken and articulate shares a fantastic business opportunity to a small room of people. Within that room there are some who know they want to move forward, they know that they want to get into the company, but you were the one who invited them out. They will sign up and get started, and you will get paid. Congratulations your company just grew! This didn't happen because you knocked it out of the park and gave an excellent presentation. This is because you used a third *person* to speak for you. You sat and listened to the presenter just like they did!

Clear! Breathing Life, Duplication & Simplicity

You want things to be simple and able to duplicate. What many prospects won't tell you, is they are trying to envision themselves doing what you, the inviter, did to invite them, (or share every little detail with them if this is what you did). Hopefully, you just invited them to hear the information. They will likely feel much stronger about being able to just invite others, however they would likely feel very intimidated to think of themselves as presenters on day one.

If you presented the information to your prospect at the store and you told them every single detail, that's what they think they will have to do to build their business. STOP IT!!! If you're doing this, you are hurting not just your business but the whole industry.

When a prospect is considering signing up under you, one of the first things they will think before swiping their card is, can I do what he/she just did? Am I able to speak like them, present like them? If the answer is no, then they are likely not going to sign up!

Sean Gary

So how do you deal with this? YOU MUST FIND 3rd PARTY TOOLS! Use them so that everyone sounds and looks the same all while keeping it simple. People will sign up and buy into simple duplication. EVERYONE CAN DO SIMPLE!

Another way to use a 3rd Person is with a 3-Way Call. They are very popular in the industry. Using a 3-Way Call does a few things, as mentioned above. When done right, you, the friend or inviter, invites someone to the information by the way of a 3-Way Call. When the invited is listening, they are not listening to you share the information, they are listening to the 3rd Person, just as above, who shared the presentation. In this scenario, it works the same as if they presented in that room and signed up a few people, but instead, the presenter, the 3rd Party leader is presented as the expert and does the sharing. The guest doesn't look at their friend or the inviter and say you don't know what you are talking about. That listener is listening to the 3rd Person leader share. More success is reached in this industry when using 3rd Party Tools, and when using 3-Way Calls.

The Desire to Help Others

This industry is one where we deal with people all the time. We have already begun to call them prospects. The next section will describe the two kinds of prospects that we deal with. When untrained and dealing with new prospects, it may become frustrating. There are meeting cancelations or delays etc. that can become exasperating. To help stay focused on our mission, which is helping solve problems for our prospects, its best to have a desire to help others.

We should be in business to answer those prospects prayers, if you will. We should help them find solutions to their issues, as we discussed before. When we have a real desire to help other people, then we will be excited to help them with those issues. What a feeling it is to have a happy customer. It's an amazing feeling; the feeling that now life will be better for the prospect. Better not just because I was able to meet them and build a new relationship, but

Sean Gary
because I was able to provide a solution for them and they honestly

felt that I and the product or service I came with, was of real value.

Cold Market Vs. Warm Market

There are two kinds of prospects. One type of prospect is the prospect whom you already know. You have hundreds and even thousands of people that you personally know. It may be hard to believe at first, but the reality is that we know a crazy tremendous amount of people. We may not have stayed in contact with them over the years, but they are still someone we know.

When you think about your teachers growing up, your classmates, your best friends from kindergarten all the way up into adulthood, you will find hundreds of people. Also, think about the sports teams you played on, the travel teams you played on, tried out for and some of which you even starred on, you can think of hundreds of people.

Maybe you were in a lot of extra-curricular clubs. Perhaps you never played sports at all, but you were in the drama club or on a dance team or you may have been a boy scout or girl scout. These

Sean Gary

individuals are all considered your Warm Market. A better way to describe your Warm Market is your "Friends and Family".

The other kind of prospect is a stranger. The person you ran into at the grocery store. The server at the restaurant, possibly the cab driver who drove you there. Better yet, your Uber or Lyft driver. These are the people that you never had a previous relationship with. They don't know you, and you don't know them. These strangers that we pass by every day easily outnumber the Warm Market because we pass by more strangers in a day than we do friends and family. This group of prospects is considered your Cold Market.

The idea of Network Marketing thrives because traditional companies pay, for example, $1 Million in advertising for a commercial, just hoping it would influence or persuade someone to buy that companies products or services. In Network Marketing, those dollars are not spent on any advertising at all, the best marketing is "word of mouth". So instead of paying money in advertising hoping to get some sales, they only pay when they already receive the sale. They pay out commissions to the affiliate who shared the company with that new customer, who was in their Cold Market or Warm Market.

Some people believe you should build your business mainly dealing with your Warm Market because you have a relationship with those individuals. In Section 2 you get to see what its like to start your company building with your Warm Market.

I personally believe that you can tap into both the Cold Market and the Warm. This book, in Section 2, will introduce to you a system that allows you to have unlimited leads of experienced Network Marketers. I think its wiser to build a business with business owners rather than friends and family who have never owned a business or a Network Marketing business before. Friends and Family will always be around, so they will end up knowing about your business, so you will be dealing with both the Cold Market and Warm Market.

Sean Gary

Most Important FACT about Building

When you think about building your network marketing business, building your team, there is one thing that is necessary above everything else. One person may consider having the best website as their primary goal for success. Or someone may think they have to have the best business cards in the world to grow their business. These can be very helpful in the overall picture of having your business. The important goal for success is to *share the opportunity*, that's it.

If you have spent 10 days creating an extra website for your network marketing business (there should already be a duplicatable site available to you) and another 10 days finding a card company to print up your business cards, these are activities that enhance your business. Activity to improve your business is good; but sharing your company's business opportunity is BEST. That's the activity you want to focus on because it directly affects your income. The most

Sean Gary
important fact about the building is you must be sharing the business opportunity to grow your business. If you are not sharing, then you are not able to make money. Share the opportunity with a lot of people, then you can explode your business!

Ways to Share

There are two main ways to share. Let's call sharing the opportunity "exposures." You can expose a smaller amount of people in a single exposure, or you can share with a large group of people. It depends on what system your team is working.

Some systems prefer exposures with more intimate settings. This may even be a one on one exposure. This can happen at a coffee shop, a friend's home, or even online through social media or via email.

Understand If you share with 10 people, that's 10 people who may say yes or they may say no to joining your opportunity. If you share with 100 people, that's 100 people who may say yes, or they may say no to joining your opportunity. I would rather have 100 people looking at my opportunity instead of just 10.

Your company should have specific ways to share for you and your team. There are tricks and tips to sharing in different platforms.

Sean Gary
A presentation at someone's home is not the same as sharing a presentation online. There are certain rules to follow and ways to get information in front of other people. Follow the plan your company has selected or stay tuned and follow the system in the back of this book.

Towards the end of this book is a training section. In that training section you will find the way I suggest you build your network marketing business. Make sure to read all the way through so you approach that section with already having gained the knowledge in the prior sections. Like all tools and personal development, feel free to go back and read and reread and even reread again so that you can have the best chance at success!

Determine Your Goals

It is essential to determine your personal goals. Not only your short-term goals but also your long-term goals. Your short-term goals should be what you desire to accomplish in the next 6 Months. Your long-term goal should be your goal for the 5-year mark.

I like to suggest having a financial goal. It's motivating for many to use financial gain as the goal, but you may also use the size of your team to be the goal. An example of a financial goal would be: "I will be making $1,000/Month in 6 Months from now!" And "In 5 years I will be making $10,000/Month! An example of a size goal would be: "I will have 250 people on my team in 6 Months!" And "In 5 years I will have 5,000 people on my team!"

Another important factor is to make sure you can track your journey. You should have a way to measure the success of your goal. Make sure you can measure your efforts to ascertain that you are on track with your goal. You may need to make a change or an adjustment along the way, possibly a few times. In the next section,

Sean Gary
we talk about personal development and then on to duplication, which plays a significant role in your goals and the measuring I just mentioned.

Personal Development

I can't say what life's expectancy was supposed to be like for you growing up, but for me, going to college was just what you do after graduating High School. Now I have a lot that I could say that's wrong with that. But for now, I will focus on the fact that I never fully understood what happens or should be happening when we are in school and the importance of it. Looking at the surface, we can say that you attend school to get smarter, to get a degree and that degree should open a career field door, etc. The problem is that's often not how the movie plays out.

I have come to my own conclusion and that's that the purpose of school is simple. It's for personal development. I define personal development just as the art of becoming more valuable. If I am learning at school, I can use that knowledge in whatever field the information can support. Gaining that information allows me to be an asset in whatever that area or field is. When we look at our

Sean Gary

income and understand the correlation between our value and our income and how they are connected, it should help us in our pursuits of financial gain.

Jim Rohn said it like this, "...we shouldn't wish life was easier, don't wish you made more money, just wish that you were better." It is imperative to understand that if you wish to increase your income, then you need to increase the value that people associate with you when they think of you. It's that simple. You're reading this, that's a great example of you deciding to work on your personal development. I pray that there is something in this book that you receive for the first time or 10th time, that hits you in a way that helps you to think better than you did before reading it. That's how you grow. Use that information to expand!

Don't stop here. When we think about personal development, there are many things that you can do to grow. There are books, seminars, retreats, conferences, etc. Go, invest in yourself. Spend the money and meet some new people along the way. As you do this, you will grow your mind and you will grow your thinking. As you increase your personal development, you will expand the size of the canvas on which your life's masterpiece is created upon.

Focus on a steady diet of personal development. This can come much easier today, because of the technological advanced era we live in. You can gain a majority of your personal development online.

~AS YOU INCREASE YOUR PERSONAL DEVELOPMENT, YOU WILL EXPAND THE SIZE OF THE CANVAS ON WHICH YOUR LIFE'S MASTERPIECE IS CREATED UPON~

There are lots of articles online; there are many books online as well. Last but certainly not least, I feel that YouTube is a vital piece of the personal development world.

Find a routine that you can daily, preferably, but at least weekly, spend some time gaining some new information or encouragement. If you don't know where to begin search on YouTube: "TheReal SeanGary Personal Development" and subscribe to stay connected to doses of personal development that I release.

Sean Gary

~THE BEST PLACE YOU CAN EVER MAKE AN INVESTMENT IS IN YOURSELF~

The best place you can ever make an investment is in yourself! That's been true for years, and it's going to likely always be true! Don't let this be the last time that you pick up a book. If you are listening to this on an audio version, great. Make sure to continue to grow your personal development after this.

Duplication

FRANCHISE! FRANCHISE!! FRANCHISE!!! I say that three times because I need you to understand that a small franchise is exactly what you just purchased. With a vast franchise, you can spend millions of dollars to get started. One of the best parts about a franchise, however, is that you have tools and systems designed and explicitly delivered from corporate and sent to you, to use, to make your franchise a success.

The same thing happens for network marketing companies. Corporate has all the tools and systems created for the field to have success. With a network marketing company, there are times when people get started and don't duplicate the system. They try to do a lot of random moves and decisions that nobody has told them to do, and no one with experience has approved. When this happens, you end up having a lot of people doing a lot of different things which

Sean Gary

makes it even harder for the team to track the successes or have any at all.

If a team of 5 people is sharing a different presentation and all 5 people created their presentations, it would be chaotic when it comes time to see what's working and what's not. Which presentation would the new people share if they hear 5 different versions? It would cause more confusion. It is essential to keep things simple and duplicatable.

As mentioned before, prospects will join thinking that they must do what you did to them. If your experience with them is a great one, then they would imagine their experiences would be great ones as well.

Now I don't want to confuse you. It's great to be trained and build up leadership skills, being able to connect with crowds, etc. but when it comes to the MOST IMPORTANT PART OF YOUR BUSINESS, "exposures," it's best to keep it a simple duplicatable system.

If you wanted to move a large log from in front of the road, would you want 5 powerful guys all pushing at random times? I would rather have 50 average people in unison push at the same time every few seconds.

~That's how a prospect can watch and say wow "I CAN DO THAT; IT'S SIMPLE." When everyone moves as a team, small, simple steps, everyone can grow their businesses exponentially! ~

Your team, which is a part of your business, will grow much longer and much more in-depth and will be more sustainable long-term in your company when everyone is doing a few simple things. When everyone knows what those few simple things are and can share that simple system with the next person that's exact duplication.

That's how a prospect can watch and say wow "I CAN DO THAT; IT'S SIMPLE." When everyone moves as a team, small, simple steps, everyone can grow their businesses exponentially! Everyone can help a ton of people! Everyone can have a ton of fun and then, of course, everyone can make a lot of money!

Sean Gary

Section II

Notes

Sean Gary

Clear! Breathing Life, Duplication & Simplicity

Sean Gary

Clear! Breathing Life, Duplication & Simplicity

Sean Gary

Clear! Breathing Life, Duplication & Simplicity

FAST START GAME PLAN

Congratulations on joining the winning team. This section is to help you JUMP START your business. Complete it immediately following your signing up. First you need to understand your "WHY". It's been said that if your "Why" doesn't make you cry then it's not strong enough.

When times get tough this is what keeps you focused. The main reason should be more than just monetary gain. Who or what is the reason WHY you have decided to start your company today? List your "Why" here:

_____

_____

_____

SHORT TERM 6 MONTH GOAL

My "Short Term" goal is to make $_____ a Month.

To reach my "Short Term" goal, I will spend _____ hours a day (Monday-Friday) working the system below!

Sean Gary

LONG TERM 3-5 YEAR GOAL
My "Long Term" goal is to make $_____ a Month.

To reach my "Long Term" goal, I will spend the next 3-5 years helping others reach their "Short Term" goals, working the same system below!

Clear! Breathing Life, Duplication & Simplicity

System 1: WARM MARKET SIMPLE SYSTEM

Step 1: Write down 50-72 names and their Cell Phone Numbers below.

1_____	2_____	3_____
#_____	#_____	#_____
4_____	5_____	6_____
#_____	#_____	#_____
7_____	8_____	9_____
#_____	#_____	#_____
10_____	11_____	12_____
#_____	#_____	#_____
13_____	14_____	15_____
#_____	#_____	#_____
16_____	17_____	18_____
#_____	#_____	#_____
19_____	20_____	21_____
22_____	23_____	24_____
#_____	#_____	#_____
25_____	26_____	27_____
#_____	#_____	#_____
28_____	29_____	30_____
#_____	#_____	#_____
31_____	32_____	33_____
#_____	#_____	#_____
34_____	35_____	36_____
#_____	#_____	#_____
37_____	38_____	39_____

Sean Gary

#_____	#_____	#_____
40_____	41_____	42_____
#_____	#_____	#_____
43_____	44_____	45_____
#_____	#_____	#_____
46_____	47_____	48_____
#_____	#_____	#_____
49_____	50_____	51_____
#_____	#_____	#_____

Bonus (Extra 21)

52_____	53_____	54_____
#_____	#_____	#_____
55_____	56_____	57_____
#_____	#_____	#_____
58_____	59_____	60_____
#_____	#_____	#_____
61_____	62_____	63_____
#_____	#_____	#_____
64_____	65_____	66_____
#_____	#_____	#_____
67_____	68_____	69_____
#_____	#_____	#_____
70_____	71_____	72_____
#_____	#_____	#_____

Step 2: Call Person #1 following the 3-Way Call script below.

Step 3: Repeat Step 2 with the rest of the people on the list.

Step 4: Congratulations, if you have reached step 4 that means that you have followed steps 1-3 and after reaching your 51 people you should have set

at least 30 Exposure Appointments and have Exposed at least 20 of them and signed up anywhere from 10-15 people!
Step 5: Help your 10-15 people follow through steps 1-5!

EXPOSURE RATE (FAST = CASH!!)
Get your 5 to Qualify
Get 10 to WIN
Then Monthly, Soar with 3 More!

Then go back and help your prospects do it all again!

Sean Gary

Clear! Breathing Life, Duplication & Simplicity

Scripts
3-Way CALLS

-Purpose: Schedule a meeting for an exposure.
-# of People: 3
-The People Involved: 1. ***"You"*** (the friend/connect) 2. Your ***"Upline"*** or a Business Partner 3. Your ***"Prospect"*** (your friend/connect)

System 1: WARM MARKET SIMPLE SYSTEM

You: Hey _(Prospect's Name)_ Thanks for taking my call. I hope everyone is doing well. Listen I don't have a lot of time, but I wanted to introduce you to MR./MRS. __(Sponsor)_. He's a really busy guy and I was able to hunt him down and get him for like 30 seconds on the phone. He has been expanding in your area and he asked me if I knew any sharp individuals and I thought about you!

Prospect: Oh, ok thanks!

Sponsor: Hello, __ (Prospect's Name) __ How are you doing?

Sean Gary

Prospect: I'm doing alright!

Sponsor: Great, well as __(Your Name)__ said, I was looking for some sharp, determined, coachable individuals. Is that you?

Prospect: It sure is!

Sponsor: Great. Ok, well you probably have some questions as to why I'm calling and to be fair to you and your time, I would like to sit down with you sometime this week maybe grab some coffee or smoothie. (Pause)
What does your schedule look like on this (list 2 different days that you already have available)?

Prospect: I'm free on this Tuesday!

Sponsor: Great! And what side of town will you be on, on Tuesday?

Prospect: I'll be in the _____ area.

Sponsor: Really, what time works best with you? I have an ___ and an ___ available. And guess what, I'll actually be over in that area on Tuesday!

Prospect: The ___ time is perfect!

Sponsor: Great, I look forward to meeting you.

Prospect: Awesome, I'll see you then.

At this point the Exposure Appointment is set and all you had to do was introduce the upline and move out of the way. Try to set appointments for the next 2-3 days.

When you all get there, just watch the upline. The new rep (you) are in training, so you shouldn't be saying much anyway. You are watching how the Sponsor answers questions, how they sit, stand, lean, speak. Pay close attention to them both and the interaction. Before you know it, one of your

Sean Gary
new people will be doing a 3-Way Call with you

simply following the script above.

Closing

Now that you have the information as to what you have joined, this amazing Network Marketing industry, I look forward to seeing you at the top. Now its time to put in the work in the network Marketing.

You have scripts, you have duplication, you have success simply waiting for you right now. No excuses. Now is your time!! Now imagine this with me…. Your WHY?

Is your WHY connected to time freedom, maybe for your kids? Maybe time freedom for your family? Maybe you want to be in a better place financially. Well, now that you have tapped into an industry that allows you to leverage your time and money and your efforts, imagine what it would mean when everyone on your team has this book?

Sean Gary

What would it mean if every single person in your organization was receiving 3-5 calls a day from experienced Network Marketers. If you only had 5 people on your team receiving 100 calls a month from experienced network marketers, to connect with your team, your business partners and some buy the system and others join your team!!! WHAT GROWTH WOULD THAT CAUSE!!! THAT'S 500 NEW PEOPLE EXPOSED A MONTH TO YOUR COMPANY!

Imagine having 10 people or 50 people duplicating??? If you had 100 people duplicating 1 hour a day making simple quick calls, that's over 10,000 new exposures A MONTH TO YOUR TEAM!!!!

About the Author

Sean Gary, also known as *The Success Jolt*, is a man that never quits. He's built a name for himself in the Network Marketing or Multi-Level Marketing profession over the past 12 years. He has trained hundreds and thousands on the secrets of team building and creating systems for success!

Not just using his Bachelor of Business degree to educate at the collegiate level while still in his twenties, he also used his personal experiences gained while owning multiple companies, to bring flavor and excitement to the classrooms and to the training field. He uses his Master's degree in Christian leadership not only in the day to day activities with his team, but he works with multiple companies to make sure their field presence is strong, educated, thriving and developing daily.

Sean builds relationships with top million-dollar earners, CEO's and other successful entrepreneurs and connects their success along

Sean Gary
with his own. Then he breaks it all down and simplifies it. This book is a curtain removed exposing one of Sean's greatest, simple systems, that anyone who joins the wonderful world of "MLM" industry can have immediate success with in today's technologically advanced era!

(Learn more about Sean at www.seangary.com)

Need a Speaker?

or

Want Sean to Train Your Team or Company?

Book Sean Gary *"The Success Jolt"*

at Your Next Event!

Email: Seangary@superiorselfllc.com

Online: www.SuperiorSelfLLC.com

Sean Gary

Clear! Breathing Life, Duplication & Simplicity

A Superior Self Production

Superior Self LLC

www.ingramcontent.com/pod-product-compliance
Lightning Source LLC
Chambersburg PA
CBHW071424220526
45469CB00004B/1414